S0-AQM-631

A SMELL OF FISH

A SMELL
OF FISH

Matthew Sweeney

CAPE POETRY

Published by Jonathan Cape 2000

2 4 6 8 10 9 7 5 3

First published in Great Britain in 2000 by
Jonathan Cape
Random House, 20 Vauxhall Bridge Road,
London SW1V 2SA

Random House Australia (Pty) Limited
20 Alfred Street, Milsons Point, Sydney,
New South Wales 2061, Australia

Random House New Zealand Limited
18 Poland Road, Glenfield,
Auckland 10, New Zealand

Random House South Africa (Pty) Limited
Endulini, 5A Jubilee Road, Parktown 2193, South Africa

The Random House Group Limited Reg. No. 954009
www.randomhouse.co.uk

A CIP catalogue record for this book
is available from the British Library

ISBN 0 224 06067 8

Papers used by Random House are natural,
recyclable products made from wood grown in sustainable forests;
the manufacturing processes conform to the environmental
regulations of the country of origin

Typeset by Palimpsest Book Production Limited,
Polmont, Stirlingshire
Printed and bound in Great Britain by
Creative Print and Design (Wales), Ebbw Vale

FOR MY PARENTS

Only the billowing overcoat remains, everything else is made up.
                                        Franz Kafka, *The Diaries*

CONTENTS

ACKNOWLEDGEMENTS

Acknowledgements are due to the editors of the following:
Agenda, Carapace, Independent, Last Words (Picador), *London Review of Books, Long Train Rising, Metre, New Writing 8, New Writing 9, Poetry London, The Poetry Porch, Poetry Review, Princeton University Library Chronicle, Salt, Stand, Sunday Times, Thumbscrew, Time's Tidings* (Anvil).

'A Smell of Fish' was commisioned by the 1999 Salisbury Festival. 'Wading' was commissioned by the 1998 Norwich and Norfolk Festival, in response to a piece of music by John Woolrich. The version of Dante, 'In the Ice', was commissioned by *Agenda*. 'The Thorpeness Poems' were written during a residency at the 1998 Aldeburgh Poetry Festival.

'The Thorpeness Poems' were published seperately in a limited edition by The Inky Parrot Press, with illustrations by John Ross.

Grateful thanks are due to the Arts Council of England for a 1999 Writers' Award.

THE ATTIC

I've finished my mural of you naked,
and only I will see it.
The sun streams through the skylight,
lighting your face, your breasts.
I lie in the hammock remembering
the afternoon hours I spent with you
up here, where no one goes.
We'd have Van Morrison singing
low down, and sometimes wine.
Always there'd be a vase of flowers
in the corner, on the trunk –
you'd smuggle them up the stairs
until you closed that black door
and the rest of the house wasn't there.
I remember the day we fell asleep
until they came looking for us –
my mother calling my name,
but not coming up. We waited
till all was quiet, then reappeared
in the living room, and sat apart,
like we had to, for half an hour –
the longest you spent down there –
then I went with you to the door.
I wouldn't accompany you to the busstop,
instead went back upstairs
to lie there in the growing dark,
listening to Van over and over again.
I must have known you'd never return.
It was weeks before I started the mural,
and I took my time, I wanted *you* there,
on my wall, right in every detail,
looking as if I could lift you down.
I wanted you, and now I've got you

and you'll never go downstairs.
Tomorrow I'll paint a vase of flowers,
irises, to match your eyes,
but tonight I'm sleeping here,
the first night I'll have spent with you.

THE HOUSEBOAT

'Did Dick Blackstaff do it?
Is he the fucker we want?'
We banged on the hatch of that houseboat,
under a blood-red moon,
while a police siren weaved among the flats
and a dog howled till a shot rang out.
But we heard no sound from the cabin,
no whisper, or muffled step,
so we banged again, and shouted
'Blackstaff, if you're in there
come out and clear your name.'
And these words rang over the water
to the wreck of the tanker
where the kids hung out in summer
but now was as bare as a crag.
And the houseboat rocked, as the wind
whipped up the incoming tide,
and brought with it the smell of curry
from 'The Star of Malibar'.
'Tell Blackstaff there's a bullet
waiting for his skull,' we shouted
before jumping back to land
and cramming in Jack's Audi
for the short ride home.

WEDDINGS AND FUNERALS
Or poem beginning with a line by John Hartley Williams

In those days I didn't go to weddings.
All that noisy drinking got me down
and chicken and ham with mushy vegetables
was best eaten once a year at most.
I hated the homegrown country music
that dragged everyone to the dance floor,
and even more the yelps and squeals
when the bride was twirled by the groom,
but worst of all was the leering question
when was it going to be my turn?

No one asked that at the funerals
I took to hunting out and attending,
and the black jacket and jeans I wore
got nods of approval and sad smiles.
I loved the stately walking rhythms
as we shuffled after the coffins,
inside of which were mostly strangers,
and I always managed a graveside tear
which earned me a beer and a sandwich
in the hotel later, where no one danced.

THE TUNNEL

When they opened the manhole
on the street outside our house
I wanted to climb into it.
I could hear the rats calling.
I could hear the smugglers
manhandling kegs of ale.
I could hear the engine
of a midget U-boat
making inroads from the sea,
and behind it, whispered German,
what these bored submariners
were saying they'd do.
I knew the tunnel went on
down the length of Ireland
and I could row for weeks
in my homemade dingy
before I'd hit the southern coast,
with my strapped-on torch
getting weaker, my water
and sardines running out,
but already I could see
the walls lightening, hear gulls
at the tunnel's end, then the strange
accents of Cork fishermen
who stood and watched me emerge.

THE LAKE

The man stood at the edge of the lake
at dawn. Behind him, in a field,
a scarecrow's rags fluttered in the wind
while a sleepy owl gave a last call.
The man stood there, as if made out of stone.
Only he could have told he was blind.

It was a lake like this had made him blind,
a similar-sized, though much warmer lake
in a province ruled over by a stone
god who'd stood in a sacred field,
and who'd banished, forever, the wind
that ancestors had said used to call –

and when a big wind comes to call
it takes the houses away. Being blind
he could easily see this, and the wind
was red, not like this northern lake-
wind that came over the grassy fields
with all the colour of grey stone.

The man bent down and picked up a stone
which he threw in the lake. A call
echoed out over the water and fields,
long and plangent. It isn't easy being blind
and standing at the edge of a lake
in a cold and unseasonable wind,

standing there, wishing you could wind
back to days when you *saw* the stones
you threw in a very different lake,
to the screeches of monkeys, the calls
of parrots – the reckless, blind
assumption that days in the fields

would always be like this, and fields
would stay bare and brown, no wind
buffeting scarecrows, a god of stone
that didn't save you from going blind
because of a worm that swam in the lake,
and a mother that rushed to your wild calls.

The man stood there. Behind him, fields,
winds away, he heard those wild calls
when his eyes turned blind, turned to stone.

WADING

She's in the sea again.
She's got her white dress on.
She's wading through the waves
watched by no one.
The stars are blotted out
and the moon's hidden,
and she's splashing through the sea
thinking about him.

He was here an hour ago.
He ran along the beach.
He shouted out 'Julie!'
and waved a torch
but he never came her way
and she ignored him,
stood there and watched
as he staggered home.

Her eyes are pebbles.
Her dress is seaweed.
Her legs are driftwood
that needs to float,
but for now she keeps wading,
slicing the waves
that keep on offering
their myriad loves.

THE APPOINTMENT

After he'd crossed seven borders
on trains, in cars, on foot,
and each language he heard
meant less to him than the last,
he came to a wooded lake,
and he knew, looking at it,
that in winter it froze over,
that people walked across it
to the island in the middle
where bonfires were lit
and dozens danced and sang
to fresh-made music,
laughing amid the snow –
he knew, because he'd seen this
in a recurring dream,
and he'd been among them
dancing alone.

And now he'd come here
but not in winter,
so he jumped in and swam,
and a red-tailed hawk
led him to the island,
where among the silver birch
he found a lantern
and a two-stringed guitar
which he practised on
till he plucked out a jig
that set his feet tapping
and got him singing,
louder and louder,
out across the water
to the listening town –
when he lit the lantern
he knew the boats would come.

THE VOLCANO

When they phoned to tell us
the volcano was finally erupting,
we threw a few things in a bag –
your best sari, my Armani suit –
grabbed the monkey and ran.
For a minute the car wouldn't start,
then we were off, rattling
down that mountain road, the stench
of sulphur in the air, you
whitefaced and silent at the wheel.
When you took a corner too quickly
and the car nearly turned over
the monkey started screeching,
so I crooned that country song
it loved, turning to look behind me
to see if lava was following
but all I saw was
a herd of donkeys, galloping,
and the sky filled with crows,
as if the mountain was emptying
of all its creatures, and all,
including us, would get away.
And as you slowed down
I put my hand on yours and squeezed,
thinking of the lava
entering our house
and swarming over the chairs,
turning them into sculptures
that one day we'd come back and see.

A DAY IN CALCUTTA

The flesh of the Indian mango is red
    like a pawpaw
but the taste is all mango.
I had it for breakfast one morning
    with watermelon juice
in that sumptuous hotel in Calcutta
    before heading off
in one of those 50s Rovers
through the crazy beeping streets
    to visit the temple
of Kalighat. It was early
    but already
there were plenty of would-be guides,
the least insistent of which we chose
    to lead us
barefoot, into Kali's sanctum
    where hands pushed us
up to her idol (black goddess
with fierce red eyes, looking as if,
    despite being stone,
she could tear us into pieces),
    as ochre marks
were thumbed on our foreheads
and offerings were requested,
    More, more
you rich Westerner! . . . Eventually
    we were outside
and heading back to our shoes
when I saw, in a crowd of men,
    two tethered goats,
one young, one a baby, both
    big-eyed and curious,
especially the eldest, until grabbed

at both ends, his neck stretched,
    then a flash
of a knife and his head was in the dust.
    The younger's bleats
were cut short in the same way,
and both bodies were dragged
    over the ground
(getting blood on my feet) and away.
    I shrugged off
the demands for money, caught up with
the others, and climbed back in
    the 50s Rover
to join the maelstrom of traffic again,
    the constant beeping
and weaving across lanes,
the certain collisions avoided,
    jaywalkers dodged
with that special skill that's the mark
    of Calcutta,
till I ended up in the leafy calm
of the British cemetery, where the Raj
    has never ended,
or so I thought, until I strolled –
    reading the names
and epitaphs – to the far end
where Indian boys were playing cricket
    among the tombs.

THE HORSES
Or poem beginning with a line from Kafka's Diaries

A herd of horses broke out of the enclosure
and galloped furiously down the dusty road.

Their leader was a sleek black stallion
with one white star gleaming on his brow.

At the edge of town they clattered onto tarmac,
tore past the church like a flooding river,

then, without slowing down, squeezed closer
to surge between the banks of parked cars.

Anyone caught driving put the boot down
on seeing that lot crowding the rear mirror

and one fat man who couldn't cross in time
felt a hoof burst his belly before he fainted.

The last in the stampede was a skinny colt,
increasingly adrift from the others,

but who still kept going, through red lights,
game as any straggler in the National,

and no one stood on the pavement with a lasso
trying to stop this last one from fleeing.

By the time the colt passed the bingo hall
the stallion had progressed beyond the graveyard

and soon all that was seen of the herd
was a cloud of dust moving above the foothills.

The too-quick dusk took away even that
and the search was called off a week later.

THE FLIES
i.m. Miroslav Holub

The flies were dying that day.
I found the first one in my hair
as I sat in the train from Cambridge,
and when I lugged my bags
through King's Cross Station
I had to stop and brush away
a fly who'd picked my face
as the last place to land on.
A third fell on my head
at the taxi-stand, and then I knew
they were dying for you, Miroslav,
or you were each of them,
pestering me, to prove you'd died,
eaten by that swift,
fleeing from the fires of Estrées.

THE TOMBS

Looking over the tombs at the cathedral,
listening to the ringing of the bells,
I see again *The Resurrection, Cookham*
only this time it's moving, not still.
I watch my granny climb out of one tomb,
younger than I ever saw her, and slimmer,
brushing the dust from her breasts,
looking round for someone to talk to.
And there, suddenly, is pregnant Doris
with the red marks gone from her neck.
And that has to be my father-in-law
standing with my grandfather, eyeing
the cathedral wall, both smoking
untipped cigarettes, till Raymond Tyner
calls them, in his drawl, to follow him
under the yew trees, out of sight,
and I rush down the stairs to meet them
but there's no one between me and the tombs.

ZEPPELINS

Landing a zeppelin wasn't easy.
You couldn't do it alone.
You needed a hundred men
running around on the ground,
grabbing the mooring ropes
that dangled down. But sitting here
on the site of the giant hangar
where those airships used to hide,
it's easy to imagine watching
until the crew climbed down,
braving backslaps and handshakes
till they made it to the mess
and wet their moustaches with beer.

And if you look they're still here
flattened into photographs
next to models of their crafts,
with one broken propellor
that brings us back to then,
to different wives or husbands,
children who ask in German
when the war's going to end,
and who point to the zeppelins
floating in the skies,
like great slow wasps,
asking, again and again,
'With those, how can we lose?'

FRANCE

In the middle of cooking an Indian meal,
he remembers a summer night in France –
the stars were falling through the sky,
and the day's premonition had been hailstones,
big as mothballs, denting the car.
Whether that was a cause or not, they'd had
a row to remember, or forget, after
the meal – *magrets de canard*, marinated,
sizzled on the barbecue, served pink –
then the recriminations started,
flying around as mad as the stars above,
and as this continued the toilet gave way,
raining unclean water through the ceiling,
while shouts echoed, till she retired,
leaving him to sit there in the garden,
in the clammy night, on the cognac now,
replaying every harsh word she'd said
while the stars got sense and settled overhead.

GUARDIAN OF THE WOMEN'S LOO
IN WATERLOO

Centimes, francs – I've a drawer full of them.
I'm not supposed to take them but I do.
At least they pay, these French women.
They don't stand there, smirking, saying
I'm broke, I'm going to wet myself,
or worse, vaulting over the metal bar
to run and lock themselves in a cubicle.
As if I'd leave my seat to stop them!

The things that go on behind me, sometimes –
sex, drugs-dealing, even a murder, once.
It's not my job to police the joint.
That's Angela's territory, when she's here.
More often than not she's doing the rounds,
but I like it when I get to talk to her,
hear her gossip, who's bonking who
in the disused waiting room on platform 12.

Sometimes she calls me back to show me
what's been left behind – knickers,
puke, a used condom (I let no men in!)
a lipstick-smeared photo of Brad Pitt.
Once there was the name Steve in blood
all over the back of the door, but the saddest,
the one that stayed with me, was a dead baby
propped up in the corner, wearing a bow.

I tell you, I want out from time to time.
The Eurostar's just across the platform,
I could go to Paris and not come back,
lose myself in Montmartre, an artist's flat
overlooking steps, but who'd take over, who'd be
guardian of the women's loo in Waterloo,
with all the tact, let live, let go by, that's needed?
10p entrance? That's half of it. The skill's in the rest.

MY DAUGHTER AND RAY DAVIES

She's going out again to that pub in Muswell Hill,
her and that bass-guitarist boyfriend of her's,
and she's wearing those red velvet hipsters.

It's not the 134 she's taking, it's a time-machine.
Look at her hair, it's a disgrace. Mods are gone,
I say, but she smiles. She's on her way to Ray Davies.

I don't know what he sees in the pair of them,
or why he listens to tapes of the boyfriend's band –
him, the writer of 'Lola' and 'You Really Got Me'.

Her room is a Kinks' shrine – all my records
nicked, and pride of place on the wall,
a blown-up photo of the three of them together.

She knows I'd love to come on the bus with them,
go down with Ray (and maybe Dave) to his local,
chat about the 60s, about the bands then,

but even though I'm younger than Ray, it's not on –
might as well try to get into the boyfriend's band,
so I sneak back my Kinks records while she's gone

and play them so loud the neighbours complain,
while she's laughing at Ray's latest jokes,
knocking back the cider to his whisky and beer.

OUR RESIDENT

Hiding the gun
in the half-full laundry basket,
he takes the stairs two at a time
to the front door.
Another long double ring,
then he has it open.
No, it isn't a constable
nor is it his wife home,
saying she forgot her keys.
It's a perfume salesman
in a lime-green jacket,
whom of course he invites in.
Seated on the sofa,
the glass table pulled up,
the man spreads his wares
while our resident makes coffee,
whispering to himself
in the blue-tiled kitchen.
He peers in at the stranger,
closing one eye, and thinks
what a mess the blood would make
of the sofa, and how would he
dispose of the body.
The first pleasant pong
distracts him, then they're all
sprayed, one by one,
on his hands and ingested
till the coffee tastes
of perfume, and he gets
his chequebook and buys
five at the special price,
then accompanies the man
to the door of the flat

where the laundry basket sits,
and it would be simple
to shoot him in the back
going down the stairs,
but the gun stays buried,
our resident has decided
its first shot will not be yet.

FIVE FIGHTERS

Strung out on the neon horizon,
the five fighters approached,
two to the left, two to the right
and one above Canary Wharf.
The searchlights and sirens were obsolete
or not yet updated, and no one
could make out the fuselage markings
so couldn't know where they came from
or why they were here,
as they cut across Southwark,
crossed the Thames for the second time
to buzz the Houses of Parliament –
policemen running, sirens bansheeing
but no tracer from rattatting guns.
Then they banked and veered to the north,
past Covent Garden and Holborn,
past Hackney and Chigwell
into deepest, darkest Essex
where they disappeared into the sky,
and none of those who'd seen them
was sure anymore, but who
wouldn't have visions of the night
the five fighters swooped on London,
flew into the centre and out again
without one of them firing a shot?

LONG DISTANCE

At the fifth ring, just as the ansaphone clicks in,
I drop the groceries, the clanking bottles, and grab the phone.
'Ah, Herr Sweeney, endlich sind Sie da!'
German! I haven't heard those sounds in some time.
I send a message to my voicebox to dredge up
a few sentences from the sub-spittle debris of what's gone
but while I'm waiting, that German voice speaks again:
'Hören Sie mich nicht, Herr Sweeney? Was ist los, Mann?'
'Entschuldigung,' I splutter, 'Mein Deutsch ist verschwunden.'
'Quatsch!' barks the firm male voice, 'Sie sind nur faul.'
And I nod, as the creaky translation filters through.
Once, for three brief months, I thought in German –
had to translate from the English I'd grown up in.
'Ja, wirklich,' I say, 'Ich bin eine Schande!'
'Stimmt,' says the cross man, 'Gut dass Sie verstehen.'
And before I can find a few simple words to reply,
'Bis nächstes Mal, dann – und ich werde Sie wieder anrufen',
then, abruptly, he is gone, no 'Tschüss',
or 'Auf Wiederhören.' I immediately press 1471 –
I want his number, want to know where he's rung from,
but *the caller has withheld his number* is what I get,
so, shaking, I replace the receiver and go straight out again.

BLUE TRAIN

Standing in the soggy queue,
waiting for the piper to arrive
and lead us to the station
where we'll board a train for Vienna,
a special blue train,
with a small original Picasso
in every compartment, and no
stops for strangers to join,
no police to scrutinise passports,
only the finest Czech beer
free in the restaurant car,
and *Wiener Schnitzel, Apfelstrudel,*
and smiling young women
fluent in three languages
to bring you what you need.

But the piper is late, and the rain
is increasing, and I've only
Czech money, and I can't shake off
the image that hijacked last night –
a couple doing it, on a bench
in full view of anyone
who chose that park to walk through
as I did – it wasn't late,
and they didn't care – so now
I need that blue train
to spirit me south, away from
Prague and its appetites,
the young in one another's laps,
clothes in disarray, but no train
will wait on the platform all day.

SOUP

We're a long time waiting on the soup.
It begins to look like we won't be served
by that half-blind, albino waitress
who took our order an hour before,
while the jazz combo took a break
and we argued about the Czech Republic.

I alone have been to the Czech Republic
where all that's edible is Gulasch Soup
(though keep that quiet or a Czech will break
a pils bottle over your head, and it'll serve
you right – don't judge before
you see for yourself) Ah, the waitress . . .

Don't just sit there, grab the waitress.
Tell her you love the Czech Republic,
tell her you're moving there before
the year is out, and ask about the soup,
our Gulasch Soup, that she will serve,
or I will, to give her a break –

anything, to give our hungers a break.
Still, it can't be fun being a waitress
whose whole purpose is to serve
in a culinary embassy of the Czech Republic.
I bet she loathes Gulasch Soup,
especially since she loved it before.

That gang over there got served before
us! Come on, give us a break –
all we ordered is six bowls of soup.
Look, we're smiling at you, waitress.
We're nicer than anyone you've served,
none of them have been to the Czech Republic,

none of them praise the Czech Republic
like I do – I wasn't being rude before
about the cuisine, I wasn't served
any humdingers on that 3 day break
in Prague, by a variety of waitresses,
except for an excellent Gulasch Soup.

And where's our soup in this Czech Republic's
watering hole? Serve us, break this embargo,
waitress, please, we've begged you before.

REBEL

Under the glass canopy
the boy climbed up the pole
while the red spotlight
stuck to him, like an aura
the whole crowd below him
could feel. And one woman
kept closing her eyes
and digging her nails into
the hand she was holding,
but the man was smiling
and urging the boy on
as the crowd were roaring,
and flashbulbs were popping,
capturing the pictures
for tomorrow's front page –
and what flag was that
held in the boy's teeth?
Why were police sirens
adding their serenade?
And how had this crowd
got past the security
and smuggled the boy in?
What, that wasn't shooting?
Who were they protecting,
the police? Ha, they missed,
and the crowd wouldn't let them
shoot again. He was at the top,
the boy, jamming the flag in,
the rebel flag, the new republic's –
a blue circle on a red square,
and the crowd erupted
as the boy jumped down
into the arms of the hundreds
and the many thousands outside.

THE ZOOKEEPER'S TROUBLES
for Tom Lynch

Riesfeldt, the zookeeper, was troubled,
so after work, when the rain cleared,
he took himself out to the orchard
and walked there among the appletrees,
in the dreamy silence that precedes dusk,
thinking of the problem that haunted him.
Why hadn't he stayed a rose-gardener?
Roses didn't need regular habits,
but his buck-elephant, Stefan, did
and, despite the soul-food of berries
figs and prunes, by the bushel,
and twenty two doses of laxative,
Stefan's private complication persisted.
For Riesfeldt's wife it was a sport,
for him it was an incitement to violence,
but he rode this, he was a survivor,
and brought to work the next morning
an abundance of extra-virgin olive oil
which he administered in an enema.
He was not prepared for his success –
the sheer force of Stefan's defecation
knocked him to the ground, his head
hitting a rock, and he lay there
while two hundred pounds of dung
formed a mountain on top of him.
It took hours to clean up the remains.

THE LETTER
Or poem beginning with a line by Keats

Before he went to feed with owls and bats
he wrote a letter to his grandmother,
asking who could stand this new stepfather
whose first act had been to kill the pets
he'd kept inside – the half-blind vole
that lived in his schoolbag, the white moth
he'd replaced once a week, the sloth
his poor Dad had brought him from Brazil,
the green Indian parrot that couldn't speak,
the hedgehog he'd saved, the scorpion
he'd smuggled from Morocco on the plane –
all dead, except the banded rattlesnake
he told his gran was hidden in the shed
waiting to be slipped into that bed.

ANIMALS

A narrative is all right so long as the narrator sticks to words
as simple as dog, horse, sunset.

Ezra Pound

Admit it, you wanted to shoot that dog
who stood barking on the edge of town,
right from the start of sunset, until
the clock in the square struck twelve
and the hotel's horse started to whinny,

sending you out from your musty bed
to the window that you flung open,
before sticking your head out and shouting
in bad French 'Fuck off, animals,
some of us are trying to sleep here!'

At that, the dog barked louder, faster,
and the horse galloped round the field,
and a rooster, fooled by the noise,
began crowing, and two cats fought
openly, on an adjacent wall.

Closing the window was all you could do,
that and turning on the shower until
the animals were lost in the hiss,
and you slept there on the bathroom floor
till light brought the squawking of gulls.

ROADKILL

Scrape the cat off the road,
take it home and fillet out the flesh,
throw it in the marinade
where the deer you wrecked your bumper on
a week before Xmas, sits
in chunks, alongside slivers of fox,
a boned, de-spined hedgehog,
the legs and breasts of a slow hare –
all in a bath of red wine
with onion slices and garlic,
and an ounce of juniper berries.
That cat was the last ingredient
you didn't know you needed
and had better keep secret.
After a day, strain the marinade
and cook the meat all morning
in the wine and blood.
Serve in bowls, with bread.

CLEAN

After a fortnight
of maggots the stink was gone
from the dead camel.

THAW

When they melted the
huge icicle a dodo
fell onto the floor.

HOBBY

I catch jellyfish
and leave them on the tarmac
to swim in the rain.

THE MOTHS

Or poem beginning with a line by Diane Di Prima

In the snow the moths walk stiffly,
they don't even try to fly.
Their footprints fill in as they make them,
as they follow one another home
up the cold poles of streetlamps
to wait there for the light.
Each dusk there's less of them,
and all more tired than before
but still they raise their voices
to greet the glowing filament –
first orange, then yellow
like their eyes. And the snow
gathers on their folded wings,
making them heavy, making some
fall to be crunched under boots,
or eaten by a passing dog,
while behind them, more walk stiffly
following the dead ones home.

ABANDONED

After two days he knew they were lying,
they wouldn't send anyone to rescue him,
he was stuck here, forever, on the moon
without even a dead man for company.
Why did they load so much dust and rocks
the module couldn't lift off?
How many experiments could they do?
How long before he'd replace some of the dust?
He looked up at Earth where his wife was.
What would they say to her? More lies,
he knew. His children would never learn
he hadn't died in a meteor shower,
and neither of them would visit his grave.
He wouldn't even have a grave!
He countered this by thinking back
to the last time he and his wife
had made love, to the borsch she'd cooked
that night, the vodka they'd drank.
What was she doing now? Did she
know he was beaming thoughts at her
across the thousands of miles of space,
hoping that in her sleep she'd beam some back?

SIPPING FRASCATI IN CASTEL GANDOLFO
for Padraig Rooney

Arriving by seaplane on the lake
down the hill from Castel Gandolfo,
you'll have time to sit in the square
with a glass or two of chilled Frascati
and sneak glances at the Pope's palace,
the two Swiss guards in the doorway
with their pikes and clownish uniforms,
and if you sit there long enough
the man himself might come out
in a sharp black suit (Armani,
not Michelangelo), dark glasses on,
the bodyguards well behind him,
and you'll nod to him as he pauses
long enough for a snifter of vodka,
then shuffles off to his regular table
at the lakeside restaurant he prefers
to any other, where they cook
what he requests the previous night,
and where no one approaches him
except the *padrone's* daughter
who reads him the poems of Goethe,
three an evening, then he signs
to the minders it's time to leave,
and soon he's back at the palace,
and if you're still sitting there
you can toast him as he goes in.

HANGOVER

Look, a drunk lying
in a canoe, being walked on
by a pair of skunks.

IN VAIN

The blind man's dog saw
the falling tree, stopped and barked,
but the man still died.

REQUIEM

Mournful music seeped
out through the window of the
overturned lorry.

A SMELL OF FISH

A smell of fish filled the valley
and all the seagulls came inland.

Cats ran everywhere, sniffing.
Men checked the level of the sea.

Some could be heard hammering.
Churches filled to pray for wind.

DO NOT THROW STONES AT THIS SIGN

Do not throw stones at this sign
which stands here, in a stony field
a stone's throw from the sea
whose beach is a mess of pebbles
since the sand was stolen for building,
and the few people who dawdle there,
rods in hand, catch nothing,
not even a shoe – might as well
bombard the waves with golfballs,
or wade in and hold their breath,
or bend, as they do, and grab a handful
of pebbles to throw at the sign,
and each time they hit it they cheer
and chalk up another beer, especially
the man who thought up the sign,
who got his paintbrush and wrote
'Do Not Throw Stones At This Sign'
on a piece of driftwood which he stuck
in this useless field, then, laughing,
danced his way to the house of beer.

When we were down in the dark hole
far beneath the giant's feet,
and I was still looking up the wall
I heard a voice say 'Watch out,
mind you don't tramp on the heads
of your miserable, weary brothers.'
I turned and saw I was walking on
a frozen lake – the ice far thicker
than the Danube ever gets, or Don,
so thick Everest could fall on it
without making a crack. And as a frog
sits with its head out of water
to croak, so these ghosts were stuck
up to their necks in the ice,
each making a noise like a stork
and keeping his face hidden. I saw
at my feet two melded together,
so much they had the one hair.
'Tell me', I said, 'who you are.'
They raised their faces, and cried
tears that froze at once, locking
their eyes, then they butted each other.
And one who'd lost both his ears
to the cold, asked 'Why do you stare at us?'
'Those, if you want to know, were twins,
treacherous brothers who killed each other,
but we're all treacherous here.'
Then I saw a thousand faces
turned to dogs' faces by the cold,
as, shivering, I walked through the heads
and straight into one. The shouts of it!
'What are you doing tramping on me?
What have I ever done on you?'

'Who do you think you are?' I said,
'to speak like that. Look at yourself.'
'No, who are you?' he answered,
'walking here, kicking me in the face.'
'I'm alive', I said, 'and if you want fame
I can get you it. What's your name?'
'Fame is the last thing I want.
Fuck off and don't annoy me further.
Flattery doesn't work down here.'
I took him by the hair and said
'Give me your name or I'll bald you.'
'Do if you want but I still won't say
who I am.' I tore out a handful,
then another, and he barked like a dog.
'What's wrong, Bocca?' another shouted.
Are your grinding teeth not enough for you?
What devil's making you bark?'
'Ha, you can keep quiet now,' I said,
'for despite you I know who you are.'
'Fuck off,' he answered, 'tell what you will
but tell about that fucker who spoke, too –
say you saw Buoso in the place
where the sinners are sent to freeze,
and if you're asked who else was there
you can name a certain Papal Legate
whose throat Florence slit,
also one Gianni de Soldanier,
and Ganelon, and Tribaldetto –
traitors every fucking one.'
We'd gone on ahead when I saw
two frozen in the one hole, one's teeth
clamped on the other's head.
'What kind of show of hatred is this?'
I asked. 'What has this fellow done
to make you want to eat him? Tell me

and I'll avenge you in the upper world,
if my tongue will still be able to speak.'

(*Inferno*, XXXII, 16–139)

INCIDENT IN EXETER STATION
for Eddie Linden

He came in the door, staring at me,
like he'd known me in another life.
'I've chased everywhere after you,' he said.
'Years and years, I've been on the road,
too many to count. The train-fares,
the bus-fares, the plane-fares . . .
The least you can do is buy me a pint.'
He plonked his duffle-bag on the floor
and sat on the stool next to mine.
He looked in my eyes like a holy man,
said 'You're looking well, you've lost weight.'
His face could have done with flesh.
His hair needed a cut and a wash.
'I don't know you', I said, 'I've never,
ever seen you before.' He smiled,
the same smile Jesus must have flashed
at Judas, then his face changed
into a voodoo mask, as he shouted
'After all I've done for you!',
turning to face the roomful of eaters
and drinkers, all of whom ignored him
but I knew they classed us together,
so, seeing a train pull up at the platform,
I grabbed my hat, bags and ran,
getting in just as the train was leaving,
not knowing where it was headed,
hearing his roars follow me out
into the green Devon countryside
that I'd never risk visiting again.

WITNESS
Or poem beginning with a line by Shelley

A man who was about to hang himself
saw strange lights in the sky.
He carried on making the perfect noose
but the lights kept dancing, like fireflies.
Why didn't they go elsewhere, he thought.
They were darting so fast here and there
and making triangular motions,
and they kept changing colour, too –
first white, then blue, then red.
The man threw his rope on the ground
as the lights zoomed close, then off again
before stopping and forming a triangle
which hung there above his head,
dropping slowly, till he could make out
the black shape the lights hung beneath –
clearly, some amazing craft of the sky
sent here for him to witness,
and he crossed himself, standing there
as the lights took off again, faster
than a shout, and soon were gone
beyond the edge of the firmament,
leaving stars that were fixed
and clouds scudding across the moon,
nothing to substantiate what he'd seen
but he'd seen it, and whistled his horse
to take him the dark road home.

IN THE DARK CHURCH
Or poem beginning with a line by Blok

I enter the dark church slowly
by the sacristy door.
It was cold out there in the graveyard
where I spent an hour,
and that dog wouldn't stop howling
at the edge of town
so I decided to creep in here,
find a place to sit down.

I feel my way past the altar,
wishing for light
but I wouldn't want to be caught
in the church at night,
still, maybe a single candle
wouldn't be noticed outside –
it could always be left lit
for someone who's died.

I carry the candle with me
to the confession box,
then snuff the tiny flame out
and think of the sex
the priest hears about in there.
I sit down inside
and slide open the grille
to hear what's said.

I forgive them all,
and invite the women home,
then I hear the organ play
my favourite hymn –

In the Bleak Midwinter —
coming to me low
and as the last note sounds
I rise and go.

SWEENEY

Even when I said my head was shrinking
he didn't believe me. Change doctors, I thought,
but why bother? We're all hypochondriacs,
and those feathers pushing through my pores
were psychosomatic. My wife was the same
till I pecked her, trying to kiss her, one morning,
scratching her feet with my claws, cawing
good morning till she left the bed with a scream.

I moved out then, onto a branch of the oak
behind the house. That way I could see her
as she opened the car, on her way to work.
Being a crow didn't stop me fancying her,
especially when she wore that short black number
I'd bought her in Berlin. I don't know if she
noticed me. I never saw her look up.
I did see boxes of my books going out.

The nest was a problem. My wife had cursed me
for being useless at DIY, and it was no better now.
I wasn't a natural flier, either, so I sat
in that tree, soaking, shivering, all day.
Everytime I saw someone carrying a bottle of wine
I cawed. A takeaway curry was worse.
And the day I saw my wife come home
with a man, I flew finally into our wall.

THE THORPENESS POEMS

And if a coat-hanger
Knocked in an open wardrobe
That was a great event
To be pondered on for hours

Derek Mahon, 'A Refusal to Mourn'

WATCHING THE SEA AT THORPENESS

Wherever I go in this flat place
I see the white dome of Sizewell,
the bald head of a killer,
so from now on I'm staying home
to watch the sea at Thorpeness.

What's better than rising early
to pull the curtains back and look
to see what ships are out?
On a good morning the sea's heaving –
I've counted three ships at a time

and twenty seven in all, so far,
including a surfaced submarine
that followed a tanker yesterday
for ten minutes, then veered off
to nose towards the Dutch coast.

They mostly sail left to right
nearer to me than to the horizon,
and tend to carry, amidships,
a large, square metal frame
whose function is beyond me.

Guessing at this is a pastime
I haven't tired of, although
my first guess was the best –
a frame for a giant painting
to be lent by the Tate in St Ives.

Sometimes the sea is empty
and this agitates me, but often
if I look far to left or right
I'll spot a comforting bump
marring the distant horizon.

Mostly, though, they're nearer –
as close as the hill I saw
from my childhood bedroom,
but better, moving slyly
all the way across the window.

It's beginning to feel addictive.
Today I was up at dawn
smiling at a ship's lights,
then I lay awake for hours
speculating on its destination.

At this rate I'll expire here,
so I've prescribed a cure –
the curtains must stay closed
in daylight or darkness
and I must never touch them.

And, wearing dark glasses,
I must walk along the beach
till I round the bend to Sizewell
where I must stay all day,
then deport myself from Suffolk.

SEA DANCE
for T.H.

The sea is wild tonight,
and the darkness sitting down on it
doesn't calm it. The ships
are skulking in the ports.
Only the barnacled bones of the drowned
are flailing through waves,
doing that dance no one sees,
that rolling and twisting underwater,
and tonight's guest-spot
goes to the newest drowner –
a jumper off Dunwich cliff
on a night milder than this,
his torch left lit on the top,
his dog howling.
                              And eels
have had his eyes, and enjoyed them,
cod have nibbled his stiff flesh,
bass have bared his foot-bones
but all this only helps him –
he has never moved so freely
or heard such fierce music,
or covered so many miles
in so few hours, and who knows
where this sea will bring him,
what coast it will dump him on,
or maybe a net will catch him
but first the sea must finish
its war, let the rising sun
bounce beams off its glassy surface,
let the bones settle on the bottom
until the next storm
when the dance will begin.

SWIMMER

For the umpteenth time I looked out at the sea
but there was nothing to catch my eye,
just a man wheeling a barrow up the beach.
I looked again, frisking the whole expanse
for a ship, a boat, any floating debris
but all I saw was a cat in the marram grass
slinking towards three rabbits playing.
The waves were apologetic on the shingle,
after the excesses of the previous night,
and the sun had lit a strip of the horizon.
All the scene needed was one small boat

but stubbornly none came. Then suddenly,
a mile or so out, I saw a swimmer –
there was no mistaking that bobbing head.
I rummaged in every drawer in the house
but none held binoculars. I ran upstairs again.
He or she was still there – it was a *she*,
I decided, and she'd made this swim before.
This was a training run for the big one –
across the Atlantic. That was why
no boats were in attendance, no copters
overhead, no paparazzi on the beach, waiting.

Up above me the roofers were hammering
as if nothing was happening. I heard a laugh
and thought of the woman in the water.
She'd be tired, hungry, cold. It was up to me
to meet her with a towel, bring her back
to my radiators and a scorching coffee,
maybe a bath, if she could still stand water.
I went to the window to see if she was near
but she'd gone, there was no head there!
I ran out, and down the lane to the beach.
The sea sent small waves to break at my feet.

THE POET OF THORPENESS

He's hidden away in Thorpeness,
writing the poems he knows will make him
the Shakespeare of the new millennium,
and although he hasn't published yet,
he's read to poets, and they've gasped,
gasped, and couldn't find words.

And they rhyme, these poems of his,
and he's got 500 of them
stored away in his Thorpeness home –
if I want I can come and read them,
now, bring my takeaway curry,
he'll crack open a bottle of wine.

Those winking lights above the sea?
That's no American warplane,
that's a UFO, they've a base here –
he couldn't always write so well –
they abducted him, turned him into a genius.

It's not fair, this advantage of his.
He knows it, but can't help it,
can't blame Faber for turning him down,
and if he can't have the best
he'll have no one – could you blame him?
He's so, so far ahead of the game.

HOOVES

The sound of galloping hooves woke me,
then a high, lengthy whinny
pulled me out of bed to the window
to see a horse standing there,
his long, black head over my gate.

There was a fine saddle on his back
with no one in it. He stared up,
never taking his eyes off mine,
as if he was mine, and I'd forgotten.
I'd have to get dressed and go out to him.

I didn't know what to do with horses,
but I took a towel with me,
and water. He'd be hot and sweaty.
Maybe I should lead him down to the sea,
so he could swim for a few minutes.

As I towelled his neck he neighed
and I smelled rescue remedy on his breath,
a smell I knew far too well.
Who'd given him that? Who'd sent
him here, and for what reason?

Was I, who'd never been on a horse,
supposed to climb into that saddle,
and let him take me where he would?
It was too cold out here to think.
I needed a strong black coffee.

I couldn't just leave the horse, though.
I wanted to take him into the house
but he was too big. Besides,
what would he do if he got in –
throw himself down on the sofa?

I tried to slink off up the steps
but his big eyes, as I turned round,
made me feel like a torturer,
so I got my scarf and leather jacket,
locked the door and got on the horse.

Immediately, he swung away,
trotting to begin with, then increasing
to a slowish gallop. I clung on,
eyes closed, clutching the horse's neck,
as his hooves rang on the road to Aldeburgh.

THE BEACH AT THORPENESS

There he is, again,
setting his easel up on the pebbles.
This is his third day in a row.
How many hours does it take
to paint the sea?
It's a bit intrusive,
right in front of my window!
I've a good mind to walk by
and stare over his shoulder,
see how good his likeness is,
how well he's captured
that watery personality.

He's the second artist
I've seen on the beach today.
The first's medium was fire –
he poured petrol
on a piece of orange net,
then set it alight,
hovering over it
to pull edges into the flames,
make sure it all went.
I watched every minute of this,
and when he left
I poked the ashes with my boot.

Then there's the woman
who spends hours
filling a pram with flat stones,
or the man I thought blind,

led by a white stick,
who instead had a metal detector.
Even the fishing rituals here –
rods sticking into the pebbles,
pointing at the sky,
little black tents to sit in,
lights for continuing at night . . .
It's like I'm living in a gallery!